Mr. Winkle is a *REAL* dog, as genuine as the underdogs
he celebrates in *A Winkle in Time*. He dedicates this book to all
the world's underdogs who have struggled against long odds and
high obstacles, and who have labored humbly in the shadows
of others—not for fame or fortune, but for the love of their
work, the faith in their vision, and the good of humanity.

— Lara Jo Regan

A Winkle in Time

Mr. Winkle Celebrates
THE UNDERDOGS OF HISTORY

Created and photographed by
Lara Jo Regan

By Mr. Winkle,
as told to Michael Regan

Random House 🏠 New York

Irish Medieval Monks
7th–12th Centuries

DESPERATE SOULS WANDERING AROUND LOOKING FOR SOMETHING TO eat. Cities reduced to rubble heaps. Big, smelly packs of barbarians stomping everything in their path. That was pretty much a typical day during the European Dark Ages. Needless to say, not many folks were taking the time to go to the library—much less to build new ones.

But that's just what the Irish monks were up to. Inspired by St. Patrick, these diligent dudes spent long days and nights copying the few books the barbarians hadn't used for firewood. Printing presses were still centuries away, so the monks had to copy each book by hand, letter by letter. That is, when they weren't too busy fighting off packs of marauding Vikings trying to sack their monasteries.

These brave, humble fellows rescued much of the culture and history of ancient Greece and Rome from oblivion. They shared their books with anyone who came by their monasteries (Vikings excluded). The monks then took the books back to the wild and woolly mainland of Europe, where they built new schools and libraries, helping to mellow the mayhem and spark the Renaissance. Though the times were dark, the future turned out a whole lot brighter, smarter, and more civilized thanks to the heroic Irish monks.

Otto Lilienthal

German Flight Pioneer

1848 – 1896

SOMETIMES YOU GOTTA CRASH A FEW TIMES BEFORE YOU CAN SOAR. German flight pioneer Otto Lilienthal knew this in his bones, many of which got broken during his daring and dogged flying experiments.

Otto spent over two decades researching, designing, testing, improving, and sometimes crashing a series of hang gliders. A few of his contraptions even had flapping wings. Those didn't work too well—and they made Otto look like a giant pelican who had too much for lunch. But Otto kept at it. Finally, in 1891, he strapped himself into a new glider and flew 80 feet. Two years later, he cruised almost 800 feet!

Otto continued flying gliders and trying to launch his dream project— a motorized flying machine, or "airplane." But a glider crash in 1896 took Otto's life. "Sacrifices have to be made" was one of Otto's mottoes. And he lived it until the end.

After his death, Otto's work soared higher and higher. His success, courage, wisdom, and willingness to share his research inspired a whole new generation of fliers, including the Wright brothers. Without Otto's endeavors, we all might still be trying to get off the ground.

ROSALIND FRANKLIN

English Scientist (1920–1958)

WHEN ROSALIND FRANKLIN ENTERED CAMBRIDGE UNIVERSITY IN 1941, women weren't even allowed in the school's dining halls. But, hey, who needs mystery meat and Tater Tots when you're hankering to become a top-notch scientist?

After graduating, Rosalind joined the school's drive to solve the greatest scientific mystery of her age: the structure of DNA. Using a new X-ray technique she'd perfected through long, lonely years of work and study, Rosalind began closing in on the answer.

One night, while Rosalind was out, her lab partner Maurice Wilkins invited some other DNA researchers—Francis Crick and James Watson—to examine her work. With the help of Rosalind's awesome X-ray pictures, the pair identified the elusive double-helix structure of DNA. Most people would have been howling mad at these scamps for swiping their work. But Rosalind was excited over the discovery and all it would mean for humankind. She even published papers to help them prove the double-helix theory.

In 1962, Watson, Crick, and Wilkins won the Nobel Prize for their work on DNA. Rosalind Franklin did not receive any recognition. She had died a few years earlier, making her incligible for the award. But Rosalind remains forever eligible for our gratitude and highest praise.

Alexander von Humboldt

Prussian Explorer, Scientist (1769–1859)

MOST EUROPEAN EXPLORERS COULD HAVE USED A FEW COURSES IN obedience school before they set sail. They ran amok over their native hosts, chewing up both land and loot. Alexander von Humboldt was different. He respected the natives and spoke out for their rights. He risked his life and life savings to explore nature and enrich all of humankind with new scientific knowledge.

Leaving behind a cushy career in Europe, Alexander plunged into the mysterious jungles of South America. He spent five years paddling down rivers, stepping over crocodiles, and climbing volcanoes. He studied plants, animals, insects, weather, rocks, and people. Alexander's work changed the way we look at the world. His treasure chest of new facts and theories revolutionized several sciences, and even created a few new ones. Alexander was also one of the first to support the idea of protecting plants from extinction.

So why do so few people today know about this awesome fine fellow? Probably because instead of making a name for himself in individual sciences, he spent the last few decades of his life trying to piece together a jigsaw puzzle the size of the universe to show what all natural processes and living beings have in common. The beauty and wisdom of Alexander's journeys were so far ahead of their time, we're still trying to catch up to him.

Queen Amanirenas

African Monarch (Late 1st Century B.C.)

WOMEN RULERS WERE ALMOST UNHEARD OF IN THE LATE 1ST CENTURY B.C. And rulers who took on the Roman Empire were usually never heard from again. But one African queen took on and took out the Romans, proclaiming her integrity and independence loud and clear for years to come.

Queen Amanirenas oversaw the small kingdom of Kush in northeast Africa. The nearby Roman Empire was at the height of its power, conquering and taxing everything in sight. When the Romans seized some of her land and slapped unfair taxes on her people, Amanirenas decided to slap back. Her troops took over a Roman fort, bringing her the head of a statue of Roman emperor Augustus as booty. Augustus sent his army to teach Amanirenas a lesson and to retrieve his head. But instead, the Romans had their rumps handed to them. The turning point in the battle came when Amanirenas took to the field herself and rallied her Kushite troops to victory.

The Romans rolled over and begged Amanirenas for peace. They gave back the Kushite land and granted them a 100 percent tax cut, leaving the Kushites to run their own country. The Romans found out the hard way: Queen Amanirenas ruled!

NORTHERN DANCER

CANADIAN RACEHORSE (1961–1990)

HE WAS JUST A PUDGY LITTLE TROUBLEMAKER AS FAR AS PROSPECTIVE buyers were concerned. So owner E. P. Taylor wasn't surprised when no one at his annual yearling sale bought Northern Dancer. Saddled with the undersized, unwanted colt, Taylor began to notice how much Northern Dancer loved to run, at least on days when the feisty little fellow wasn't too busy frolicking in the snow or slip-sliding along frozen walkways.

After some intense training, Northern Dancer showed great promise as a two-year-old, winning five races with his odd, choppy stride. Still, even his own jockey, Bill Shoemaker, didn't think the tiny Canadian horse stood a chance against undefeated giant Hill Rise at the next year's Kentucky Derby. Riding with a new jockey and a cracked hoof, Northern Dancer astonished the crowd at Churchill Downs as he zoomed by Shoemaker and Hill Rise to win the world's biggest horse race in record time!

A few months and a few big victories later, a leg injury forced Northern Dancer to retire to stud. Taylor had to dig a pit for fillies to stand in so they'd be on equal footing to court his pint-sized champion. The little equine that could went on to sire so many great horses that now over half of the world's racing Thoroughbreds branch from his sprawling family tree.

Fannie Lou Hamer

American Civil Rights Activist (1917–1977)

FANNIE LOU HAMER WAS FORCED TO BEGIN PICKING COTTON WHEN SHE was only six years old. It was hot, grueling work, but one of the only jobs open to blacks in the South at the time. After 38 years of sharecropping, she found herself poorer than ever and "sick and tired of being sick and tired." Then she saw a way up from being way down and helped bring the rest of black America along for the climb.

Fannie Lou recognized that the right to vote was the key to blacks' gaining power and the chance to make a decent living. But racist laws and violent intimidation scared most Southern blacks away from even trying to register. Not Fannie Lou. She showed up at the Sunflower County courthouse in Mississippi one day to sign up to vote. She was turned away, arrested, kicked out of her home, and shot at. Later, she was jailed and beaten all night.

Though the jailhouse beating left her barely able to move, Fannie Lou kept striving toward justice. At the 1964 Democratic National Convention, she riveted millions of TV viewers with the tale of her struggles. Fannie Lou Hamer's speech generated a groundswell of support for reform. The following year, the Voting Rights Act rode that wave into law, forever washing away barriers that stood between black Americans and the polling booth.

ALAN LOMAX

AMERICAN FOLKLORIST (1915–2002)

HIS NAME WAS ALAN LOMAX, AND HE CALLED HIMSELF A "SONG HUNTER." Starting in his teens, Alan drove around the American South looking for music with a tape recorder bolted into the back of his pickup truck.

Over the next fifty years, Alan recorded tens of thousands of obscure musicians from thousands of obscure places around the globe. Songs and musical forms that might have been heard only by a few neighbors before going extinct were now relayed all over the world through Alan's recordings and radio broadcasts. New styles of music sprang up in his wake. Rhythm and blues. Rock 'n' roll. The folk and blues revivals. World music. Even the origins of rap and hip-hop can be traced in part to his work.

Some of the folks Alan discovered went on to become stars. But Alan himself preferred to toil behind the scenes. His tireless, selfless efforts were motivated by a love of music and his deeply held belief that all people were equal, each capable of great beauty, each worthy of deep respect—and that the proof was in the musical pudding.

Alan Lomax built a giant musical library from which the world continues to check out tunes every hour of every day. Kudos for his profound contributions are the only things overdue.

Camille Claudel

French Sculptor (1864–1943)

DIGGING CLAY AND STONE OUT OF THE COLD, WET GROUND. WIELDING HEAVY hammers and chisels. Working all day and night in a chilly studio, carving big blocks of marble into larger-than-life statues. If you'd asked anybody in the 19th century, they'd have told you: sculpting was a man's job.

Fortunately, Camille Claudel didn't ask. Starting when she was just a little girl, Camille plunged hands-first into the mud to shape figures that revealed a talent beyond its years and an artist ahead of her time. Through decades of practice and study, Camille continued developing her skills until she became a master of turning cold, lifeless slabs of stone into testaments to the human heart and soul.

Unfortunately, Camille never managed to sculpt out a niche for herself where that work could be seen and appreciated. The smug thugs of the male-dominated French art world of her day didn't think a woman could create worthy sculptures. Such knuckleheaded notions long ago crumbled into dust at the feet of Camille Claudel's dazzling sculptures, which still stand tall in museums around the world.

PHILO T. FARNSWORTH

American Inventor (1906–1971)

MOVING PICTURES FLYING THROUGH THE AIR INTO LITTLE BOXES?? Even today, television seems like magic. What's even more amazing? How about that the notion for this unlikely gizmo first popped into the noggin of a 14-year-old boy named Philo T. Farnsworth while working on his family's Idaho potato farm?

Philo T. Farnsworth already had plenty on his mind. The oldest of five children, he was responsible for looking after his little brothers and sisters. Each day began with a four-mile horseback ride to the nearest schoolhouse. And "homework" included helping his dad with the backbreaking labor of raising potatoes. All that didn't stop Philo from daydreaming about his favorite subject: science. One day, while tilling rows of potatoes, Philo concocted the idea of shooting an electron past rows of an image to transmit a picture through the air.

Philo put in three decades of trial, error, heartbreak, and battle with a giant corporation that tried to steal his work before he'd perfected his "television." But by then, Philo was bankrupt and convinced he could no longer compete with the big companies that would ultimately reap billions of dollars from his invention—while offering him no credit or thanks. Philo died in 1971, before he could wrap up work on his next great project: cold-fusion energy, a concept many scientists still believe holds great promise in solving the world's energy problems. By then, though, the genius of Philo T. Farnsworth was already glowing in millions of homes across the globe.

Farnovision

GREEK WARRIORS
AT THE BATTLE OF THERMOPYLAE
480 B.C.

WHAT WOULD YOU DO IF A MILLION BRUISERS WITH WEAPONS AND bad attitudes were headed your way? Or should I ask, in which direction would you run? Greece's King Leonidas chose to charge straight at them. With a humongous Persian army marching toward Greece, Leonidas led a small group of soldiers to defend Thermopylae, a narrow mountain pass directly in the Persians' path. When the Persians boasted they could fill the air with so many arrows the sky would turn black, a Greek commander shot back, "Good, then we'll get to fight in the shade."

These guys didn't just woof the woof, they kicked some serious hoof, too. The tiny Greek outpost fought off attack after attack. The Persians had to cheat to win, eventually surrounding the last 300 Greeks with the help of a traitor. Even then, the Persians wouldn't chance another charge at the gutsy Greeks. With spears and arrows raining down upon them, the Greeks fought to the last man.

The heroic stand by King Leonidas and his men gave their countrymen time to prepare for the Persians' attack and ultimately defeat them. This small band helped save Greece and the rest of Europe from Persian conquest. Most of what we now know as Western history and culture might have been ground into kibble had these gallant Greeks not stood their ground.

Saint Elizabeth of Hungary

Hungarian Benefactress (1207–1231)

WE ALL LOVE GOOD OL' SAINT NICK, BUT HE ONLY SHOWS UP TO WORK ONE day a year. Saint Elizabeth of Hungary was on the job delivering gifts to the sick and needy every single day of the year.

Life was not as good to Elizabeth as she was to everyone she met. Her mother was killed when she was only eight. In her teens, Elizabeth lost her fiancé. She eventually got hitched to his younger brother, but he died a few years later, too. Elizabeth then got tossed out of her home by her greedy in-laws, and she and her four children were forced to live for a while in a pigsty.

Beneath this burden of outrageous misfortune, Elizabeth just kept up her good works. Her daily walk included stops to give what food and money she had to 800 poor people. She turned her house into a hospital for the needy, then tended to the worst cases herself. Her visionary kindness led her to establish the world's first orphanage.

Even as she lay dying, Elizabeth thought only of others. She ordered that all her goods be donated to charity, except for one old, torn dress, in which she asked to be buried. Elizabeth of Hungary left this world with the peace of mind that comes from giving everything you've got. And the world was left with a deeper faith in the kindness and generosity of others.

MIGUEL HIDALGO

MEXICAN REVOLUTIONARY (1753–1811)

HIS LAST NAME MEANS "SON OF SOMEBODY." AND BEFORE HE WAS FINISHED with his extraordinary life, Miguel Hidalgo proved that he was somebody indeed.

A country priest, Miguel did everything with gusto—whether it was preaching, dancing, street bowling, or helping the needy. He even turned his house into a night school and factory for poor local craftsmen to help them earn a decent living. Like many of his fellow countrymen, Miguel believed that Mexico was ready for independence after three centuries of poverty and oppression beneath the Spanish colonial boot. One day, Miguel became so stoked with the idea, he ran onto his porch and called for the townspeople to join him in a revolution. Miguel spoke with such conviction and fervor, a crowd of peasants immediately gathered on the street and overthrew the town's Spanish rulers.

The revolution spread across the country, with Miguel leading an army of over 80,000 peasants to the gates of Mexico City. Armed mostly with pitchforks and passion, the rebels were finally crushed by the mighty Spanish army. Miguel was captured and sentenced to die before a firing squad. He offered candy to his executioners and instructed them to aim for his right hand, which he then placed over his heart. Even after Miguel's death, that heart kept beating the drum of freedom, rousing Mexicans to fight on for ten more years, until they finally won their independence.

HER PARENTS DIDN'T EVEN BOTHER TO WRITE DOWN HER NAME or birthday, but that was a girl's bum lot in life in 10th-century Japan. The boys got all the perks and power—not to mention the birthday parties. But Murasaki Shikibu (as she later named herself) got plenty of brains and curiosity. She even educated herself by eaves-dropping at the door as her father tutored her brother.

Murasaki married young, but was widowed a short time later. Forced to fend for herself and her newborn daughter, she took a job in the royal court. Women at court were expected to be seen and not heard. That didn't stop Murasaki from seeing, hearing, and understanding *everything* going on around her. Using her keen eye and boundless imagination, she brewed up something the world had never seen before: a novel. And what a novel!! Murasaki's *Tale of Genji* is a great big book that most scholars still consider the finest work in all Japanese literature.

It would be five more centuries before anybody in Europe thought to write a novel, and many more years before they approached *Genji*'s genius. I guess you could say Murasaki Shikibu wrote the book on how to write a novel.

MURASAKI SHIKIBU

JAPANESE WRITER

(978?–1031?)

Nathanael Greene
American Revolutionary War Hero (1742–1786)

DON'T GET ME WRONG—RED, WHITE, AND BLUE LOOK SWELL TOGETHER. But maybe we should add a touch of green to the U.S. flag in honor of American Revolutionary War hero Nathanael Greene.

Nathanael made a habit of overcoming obstacles early on. With his family unable to afford the education he longed for, Nathanael paid for his own library by crafting and selling toy cannons and anchors. He especially liked books on military history, reading every volume he could get his hands on. A bum left leg almost kept Nathanael from lending his military expertise to the American Revolution. But he just kept marching, making it to the battles of Princeton and Trenton, where he fought beside General George Washington.

Washington was so impressed with Nathanael, he put him in charge of the American forces down South. The honor was great, but this was no plum gig. America's Southern army was exhausted from years of battling the better equipped and much bigger British army.

But the British didn't stand a chance against the savvy Nathanael. In less than two years, he and his men captured all the British forts, along with thousands of prisoners, in the South. The rest of the Redcoats hightailed it north to Yorktown, where they surrendered to General Washington in 1783, ending the war and marking the true beginning of American independence.

ARAB ARCHITECTS
7ᴛʜ–13ᴛʜ CENTURIES

ALMOST ALL OF THEIR NAMES HAVE BEEN FORGOTTEN, THEIR ACHIEVEMENTS demolished, their inventions copied and credited to others in faraway lands. But for over half a millennium, Arab architects humbly led the world in discovery and innovation. With their mind-boggling use of light, fountains, gardens, domes, and intricate interior design, these ingenious engineers concocted some of history's most ogle-worthy buildings. Check out the stupendous Alhambra in Spain, Jerusalem's shimmering Dome of the Rock, or the ultra-magnificent Taj Mahal in India, then you'll get an idea of how darn gorgeous Middle Eastern cities and towns looked during the Muslim Golden Age.

Unfortunately, there's not much more left to check out. Most of the Arabs' engineering marvels were trashed by jealous Mongol hordes stampeding through the Middle East in the 13th century.

Fortunately, you can't keep a grand tradition down—even if it's been pulverized into sand dunes. Because grains of that sand blew around the world as great notions, enlightening engineers from the Renaissance to the century after tomorrow. The brilliant work by the Arab architects of the Muslim Golden Age was distilled into ageless design ideals that continue to snazz up buildings throughout the world.

Rosie THE RIVETER

1941–1945

THE GALS BACK HOME WITH THE WRENCHES RANKED AS HIGH AS THE guys in the trenches in World War II. The U.S. desperately needed fresh ships, tanks, planes, bombs, and other equipment. Problem was, most of the men who used to build this stuff were off fighting the war.

Up stepped Rosie the Riveter—the nickname for working women during World War II. The Rosies took over almost 20 million jobs in the U.S. They built the ships and planes, greased the engines, and cranked out the ammo. It was doggone difficult, dirty, and dangerous work, with almost 40,000 Rosies dying in the line of duty and over 200,000 becoming permanently disabled.

Their sweat, muscle, courage, and determination not only helped the U.S. and its allies win the war, the Rosies also lent a big hand in pulling the country out of the Great Depression. And by proving that women could get the job— any job—done, the Rosies swung open the career door for their daughters and granddaughters. Maybe when women apply for a job today, they should list Rosie the Riveter as a reference.

Laika

Russian Space Pioneer (1954–1958)

MOST DOGS SETTLE FOR A WALK AROUND THE BLOCK A FEW TIMES A DAY. The canine cosmonaut Laika didn't stop until she'd cruised dozens of times around the whole planet!

Laika was found wandering the streets of Moscow by Soviet authorities. Impressed with her sweet personality and hardy spirit, they named her Laika ("barker") and enrolled her in the country's space program. On November 3, 1957, Laika boarded the *Sputnik II* rocket and zoomed into the wild black yonder, becoming the first earth creature in outer space. Some people sneered at her heroics and called Laika's ship *Muttnik*. But you can't blame them for being green-eyed. Laika was 2,000 miles over their heads, doing laps around the planet at 18,000 mph. What a ride!

Unlike the astronauts, cosmonauts, and chimps who followed her, no hero's welcome awaited Laika back on Earth. *Sputnik II* went up, but the Russian scientists hadn't figured out yet how to bring a spaceship back down. Laika died in orbit. But she'd already taken one long walk for dogs, and one giant journey for all mammalkind.

MATTHEW SAAD MUHAMMAD

American Boxer (born 1954)

MATTHEW SAAD MUHAMMAD REMEMBERS CHASING HIS OLDER BROTHER across the bridge, calling for him to come back. But he was only five years old and his little legs couldn't catch up. It was one of the few times in his life that "Miracle Matthew" hasn't beaten the odds and come from behind.

Weeks earlier Matthew's mother had died, leaving him an orphan. His aunt couldn't afford to care for both boys, so she ordered Matthew's brother to abandon him. The police found Matthew near the bridge and put him in a foster home. But it was in a neighborhood full of bullies, who beat Matthew up on his way to school. Matthew took up boxing to learn how to defend himself.

Matthew worked out every day and turned pro when he was just 19. He got so good that five years later he landed a fight with world champ Marvin Johnson. The heavily favored Johnson battered Matthew, leaving him wobbly and exhausted by the eighth round. But Matthew just kept staggering forward and swinging, even though he could barely see. To the amazement of almost everyone, he knocked Johnson out! Matthew was now the light-heavyweight champion of the world.

Matthew defended his title eight times. He showed incredible courage, grace, and dignity during his fights, always praising his opponents and usually winning after just about everyone had counted him out. After retiring, he began teaching poor kids those same qualities. For all that, Miracle Matthew will always be a champ in my book.

A Winkle in Time created and photographed by Lara Jo Regan.
Many thanks to her gifted and passionate collaborators:

Set & Prop Design *Chris Hopkins*

Graphic Design *Mika Toyoura Mingasson*

Costumes *Fionn Zarubica*

Additional Costumes Dara Folkert

———◆———

*A very special thanks to Darryl Redalieu, a longtime friend and colleague whose
ongoing generosity, support, and enthusiasm for great lighting have never failed
to make Winkle productions more challenging, inspiring, and fun.*

*Mr. Winkle thanks all the folks at Random House for
supporting this project, especially Courtney Silk.*

Copyright © 2003 by Lara Jo Regan.
All rights reserved under International and Pan-American Copyright Conventions.
Published in the United States by Random House Children's Books,
a division of Random House, Inc., New York, and simultaneously in Canada by Random House of Canada Limited, Toronto.
www.randomhouse.com/kids
www.mrwinkle.com
Library of Congress Control Number: 2002094041
ISBN: 0-375-82487-1 (trade) — ISBN: 0-375-92487-6 (lib. bdg.)
Printed in the United States of America   First Edition   10 9 8 7 6 5 4 3 2 1
RANDOM HOUSE and colophon are registered trademarks of Random House, Inc.
Mr. Winkle and his likeness are trademarks of Lara Jo Regan.